Honestly

Honestly

Steven Zultanski

Book*hug | 2018

Book*hug acknowledges the land on which it operates. For thousands of
years it has been the traditional land of the Huron-Wendat, the Seneca, and
most recently, the Mississaugas of the Credit River. Today, this meeting place
is still the home to many Indigenous people from across Turtle Island, and
we are grateful to have the opportunity to work on this land.

LIBRARY AND ARCHIVES CANADA
CATALOGUING IN PUBLICATION

Zultanski, Steven, author
        Honestly / Steven Zultanski.

Poems.
Issued also in print and electronic formats.
ISBN 978-1-77166-410-3 (SOFTCOVER)
ISBN 978-1-77166-411-0 (HTML)
ISBN 978-1-77166-412-7 (PDF)
ISBN 978-1-77166-413-4 (KINDLE)

        I. Title.

PS3626.U58H66 2018   811.6   C2018-900360-X
                                       C2018-900361-8

PRINTED IN CANADA

Honestly

I never met my great-uncle, Dick Stryker.

But about ten years ago, while visiting family, I found his copy of Joyce's *Ulysses*; the inside cover was stamped with his name and the pages were dotted with marginalia.

I asked my parents who he was, but it had been so long since anyone had mentioned him that they could barely remember the rumors: he was a pianist and a composer; he was jailed for being a conscientious objector during World War II; he spent two years in a prison in Ohio; his father kicked him out of the family; he moved to New York; he was gay; he was an alcoholic; at some point, he burned his face off somehow; he might have been homeless for a time; he refused to have anything to do with his family.

I wanted to know more, I wanted to feel a slightly stronger mild connection to this person I'd never heard of.

At first, it was hard to find information about him; as you might expect, his name is difficult to google.

There are many Dick Strykers, and most of them are the pseudonymous authors of porn.

But I did find a brief reference to our Dick Stryker—my Dick Stryker—participating in an early production by the Living Theatre, and this led me to the published diaries of its founder, Judith Malina, which contain frequent references to Dick.

Turns out he was roommates with Malina and her partner and collaborator Julian Beck, and he wrote music for many of their early plays.

Unfortunately, the diaries don't provide many personal details, but the glimpses into the company he kept suggest that he lived an active artistic life, despite his eventual obscurity and disappearance: he hung out with John Ashbery and Frank O'Hara; he played one of the radios in the first performance of John Cage's *Imaginary Landscapes IV*; he studied with composer Lou Harrison; he wrote the score for one of Jackson Mac Low's plays, and Larry Rivers played saxophone on the recording.

I have no idea if this recording still exists—probably not, but I hope so.

He attended anarchist meetings.

He dated a poet, Harold Norse, who wrote many poems about their tumultuous relationship.

He had difficulty finding work because he was a felon.

He washed dishes.

He frequently missed attending or participating in concerts because he was washing dishes.

The most moving anecdote in the diaries is a prank: Dick and Judith attend a séance, but he won't behave.

Either he's angry at his friends or he can't take the ritual seriously; for one reason or another, he continually acts up.

He spells out evil messages on the Ouija board, and is eventually kicked out when he forms the word *hate*.

When I read this, Dick came alive to me; he felt close.

On the one hand, I simply love that he made a life so far from his conservative suburban roots, that he conjured spirits with weirdos in the East Village, participating in things that people in our family would find pointless, unproductive, and unusual; but even better, I love that he refused to play along, that he fucked it up, that he threw cold water on everyone else's optimistic spiritualism with a harmless and silly but slightly mean joke—a life-affirming kind of joke, probably funnier in retrospect.

But later in the book, he and Judith get into a physical altercation. The incident is recorded in detail in Harold Norse's memoir: backstage after a concert, Dick confronted Judith about a debt, she slapped his face, he pushed her, she tried to steal a flute from a flautist with the intention of beating Dick with it, the flautist wouldn't let go and struggled with Judith, she bit his hand until he bled, and then Dick spat on her and ran away.

It wasn't the end of their friendship; they continued to live and work together.

But a year later he moved out, and after that his name rarely appears in her diaries.

I emailed Judith.

She wrote back immediately, excitedly: she was so happy to hear from a relative of Dick's, he was a dear friend but then he dropped out of her life, she didn't know what happened to him, no one knew what happened to him, she was eager for news, she wanted me to put her in touch with him, she wanted to see him again.

I wrote back and corrected the misunderstanding: Dick had been dead for fifteen years, I didn't know what happened to him either, that that's why I had written, I was hoping she had more information, I was hoping she would share memories, I was hoping she could tell me about his personality, I wanted to know what he was like.

She didn't respond.

I asked my grandmother about Dick.

They were close as children.

He was a musical boy; he loved Wagner.

She always hated Wagner.

But she didn't know anything about his adult life; the last time she saw him was in 1948, at her wedding.

I told her that I had learned more about him, that he moved to New York and hung out with artists and writers whom I admire, people I try to copy in my own writing, people from a certain bohemian milieu considered Very Important by artists today.

She said, "But I don't know why he never came to see me again.

I don't know why he never called me.

I don't know why he never answered my letters.

I don't know why he stopped talking to me."
She repeated herself without looking at me.
She's 94, and quickly forgets what she's said.

A few years later, I attended a talk by Judith, and afterward
introduced myself as the great-nephew of Dick Stryker.
At the mention of her old friend she became flustered, told me
repeatedly how much she loved Dick and how much I looked like
him: you look just like him, I'm so happy to see you, you have his
hair, you're bringing back memories, I miss him, it's been so long,
I've missed him for so long.
I was happy to be told I looked like Dick, it made me feel like
we were linked, like there was a connection between us more
fundamental than my occasional shallow curiosity about his life—a
living piece of him hidden in me that I was about to discover.
But when I proudly relayed this story to my grandmother, she was
baffled: you look nothing like him, nothing at all, that's ridiculous,
completely ridiculous.

Eventually, I was able to track down two of Dick's surviving friends,
and they told me what they could remember, or what they wanted
to tell.
They lingered on the sad trajectory of Dick's life, though they also
made clear that he was private; there was a lot they didn't know.
I was disappointed that neither of them commented on my
resemblance to Dick.

He was a happy young man, though he had bouts of depression and an occasional tendency to self-harm.

He had lots of friends.

He drank a lot.

The fact that he had actually been to jail for his beliefs made a big impression, and people looked up to him.

He was active in the pacifist movement, and knew Bayard Rustin from political meetings.

He became interested in Gestalt psychology, and was a patient of Isadore From for a time, though nobody knows how he could afford it.

He always hung around poets, but was never interested in reading poetry.

He seems to have broken the young James Baldwin's heart.

He had some early success as a composer.

He wrote an organ passacaglia that was performed by a famous organist at Columbia University.

The orchestrated version won third prize from a music foundation, and was performed by the Chicago Symphony Orchestra in a rehearsal.

Dick's friends pooled their money to send him to Chicago to hear his music, but they didn't have enough.

At this point the story gets hazy before getting clear again.

In the late 50s, he had an affair with a poet named Murray that was so all-consuming that he stopped focusing on composition.

Murray had a wife and kids, but his wife knew about Dick and they were all close; when Murray's family moved to San Francisco, Dick moved with them.

That didn't go well, and Dick moved back to New York.

But he remained close to Murray, who died young of leukemia a few years later.

Dick visited him many times while he was dying.

After that, his love life remained unstable, though I don't know the details.

I wish I did.

I want to pry.

Then he almost died in a fire.

One of his friends told me, "The fire was probably in 1971, on Perry Street.

He was smoking and fell asleep and it started.

He tried to escape but couldn't get the bars out of his windows.

The firemen broke in and found him badly burnt and unconscious.

They said he had actually inhaled flame.

His lungs were charred.

"He was disfigured and they had to reconstruct his face.

They sewed new eyelashes on.

They built a new nose using the skin from his arm.

They attached the skin from under his right arm to his nose, and then held his arm over his head for three months while it fused with the skin on his face.

He always looked disfigured after that.

The joints in his fingers were burnt and no longer worked.

They had to cut the joints and remake the fingers.

His fingers were bent back for the rest of his life.

"He also gained a lot of weight after this, because he was not very mobile.

He spent a total of about ten months in the hospital.

The fire probably destroyed most of his scores.

When we visited him in the hospital, he was unrecognizable except for his laugh."

Unable to work, and living on disability benefits, he became a loner, refusing to see many of his old friends because he was ashamed of his face.

Mostly he stayed indoors and listened to Renaissance music.

He withdrew from social life, and rarely composed: "One of the few pieces of music he wrote after the fire was for a doctor named Dr. DeFilippi.

When he was slipping in and out of consciousness in the emergency room, he said that every time he woke up, Dr. DeFilippi would be sitting there praying for him, even though he didn't know him.

He might have credited this praying with saving his life.

Maybe it was a religious conversion.

He remained friends with DeFilippi.

Later, the doctor's wife was murdered, and Dick wrote him a piece of music as a gift, or an elegy."

A few years before he died, Dick fell down the subway steps.

The station was missing its handrails, because of construction.

He was badly hurt, and sued the city.

This money made his last few years easier, until he got lung cancer.

"He was in chemo and doing well, but then he caught a cold and died of pneumonia."

*

Moving is expensive and now I'm broke.
It's not just the cost of the truck and the boxes and the movers; and
it's not just the security deposit and the first month's rent and the
last month's rent and the modem installation fee; it's all the small
items that I'm replacing because they were lost in the move, or
that I never owned but I now feel like I should have owned, and
so am buying for the first time begrudgingly, as if I were replacing
something.

These things add up.
The shoe rack for $12.99.
The cheapest mattress I could find for $129.30.
The screwdriver for $3.99.
The ball of twine for $2.49.
The mini ironing board for $14.99.
The iron for $24.99.

And of course I rebought all sorts of toiletries and cleaning
products.
Q-tips.
Listerine.
All-purpose bathroom cleaner.
Paper towels, sponges, floss, plunger.

Hand soap.
Bleach.

$3.88
+$7.12
+$3.27
+$7.99, $5.48, $3.74, $9.99
+$2.99
+$6.99
=$51.45

I have some good friends.
For the last few months, I've slept on their couches and floors and
air mattresses.
Finally I moved into a new apartment: a tiny place, a room with no
kitchen.
But it has its own entrance.
I don't have to share, it's all mine, I can come home without saying
hello to anyone, I can drink coffee alone.
It's not big enough for guests.
There's no couch.
There's nowhere to sit except the mattress and the ergonomic office
chair and the floor.

If a friend needs a place to sleep, they can't sleep here.
If they need a place to hide, they can't hide here.

The closet is cramped.

The bathroom is narrow.

There's nothing to crouch behind, nothing to hide under.

The front door is easy to pry open.

Someone could walk right in.

Where are they?

Where the fuck are they?

I know they're here.

I know they're fucking here.

I bet you hid them behind the fucking shower curtain, right?

That's your genius hiding spot, right?

You probably thought we wouldn't look there, right, in the most
fucking obvious spot, right?

I know they're here somewhere.

So where the fuck are they?

Did you hide them in the fucking closet?

That's so fucking obvious, hahaha.

As if that wouldn't be the first fucking place we'd look, hahaha.

What is all this shit?

What the fuck are you doing buying this garbage?

Look at this shit.

A VCR?

A flute?

Why the fuck do you have a flute?

I know they're in here.

They must be in here.

You shoved them behind all this crap, right?

Ok.

Ok, now I'm getting angry.

Where are they?

You think this is funny?

You think it's funny that I smashed a plate?

It's just a fucking plate.

We can smash a lot more than a fucking plate.

We'll smash all your plates.

All your fucking glasses too.

And every one of your fucking windows.

Oh, that's not enough for you?

You want more?

You want me to tear these clothes to shreds?

We'll tear every fucking stitch of clothing to shreds.

These fucking curtains too.

Look, you'll tell us where you hid your fucking friend.

I know you will.

And you know you will.

Because I know they're here.

And you want us to leave you alone, right?

That's what you want, isn't it?

You don't want us to smash every one of your fucking plates all over again, right?

Of course you don't.

I understand.

Listen, this is what's going to happen.

We're going wait in the hall.

And while we're out there, you're going to drag your friend from their hiding place and explain to them that they're coming with us.

You can say whatever you want.

You can put it gently, be as nice as you want, I don't care.

We're doing this for you, a little favor.

We'll give you a few minutes alone with them.

We'll be waiting right here, just outside the door.

*

My friend Zach is the son of a government worker, and according
to him, the mob is not only heavily involved with real estate
developers, which you would expect, but with labor unions, which
you would also expect, though it feels good to hear someone say
it, because I never knew it for a fact and now I can repeat it with
authority.

There's a certain pleasure in having cynical knowledge confirmed
because then it no longer feels like cynical knowledge, it just feels
like your eyes were already open, which they probably were.

Not that I went around thinking about which specific sectors of the
city economy were run by the mob.

I never really thought about the mob.

But I've thought about developers.

And I've assumed, without exception, that they are all intractably
corrupt.

And I've thought about the ordinary rule of shadowy economic
conspiracy that governs all areas of city life, from the displacement
of neighborhoods for the construction of a new stadium to the
prohibitive expense of food cart licenses and the subsequent
aggressive ticketing of food carts for expired licenses.

So learning about the mob's involvement with the unions
confirmed some helplessly vague but intuitively precise knowledge,

which I assume I share with many others, about "how the world works."

My first thought was: duh, of course, I already knew that, who doesn't know that, I've known that for so long, how could anyone not know that, everyone knows that.

But Zach also told me something more interesting and slightly surprising: recently, the labor unions have built alliances with environmental activist groups in an effort to push through green legislation.

This alliance is just political, not ideological.

It's basically a marriage of convenience.

Labor wants to produce more jobs, to increase their power and influence, and the large-scale infrastructural changes necessitated by strong environmental legislation would mean a bunch of new jobs.

Since it seems inevitable that the city will eventually pass some version of this legislation, they want to be on the ground floor of the negotiations so they can make sure these are union jobs.

That wouldn't be legal, but there are workarounds.

For example, even though the law can't make the city hire union workers, it can include a licensing requirement that can only be met with a certain kind of training provided exclusively by the union.

This requirement would probably be disguised as a safety initiative packaged with the environmental legislation.

It's unclear whether lawmakers would even know what the real purpose of this safety initiative was, or if only their lawyers would know.

By the way, the unions are totally racist and sexist.
I suppose that's obvious.
Out of everything my friend said, that's the thing that least surprised me, because there's nothing blandly novel about it, no half-revelatory details about convoluted power structures, no banal intricacy of municipal machination, just an obvious fact: the members are basically all white men, and they don't hire people from the neighborhoods they're working in.
Moreover, the structure of the unions—a mix of top-down hierarchy, government and mob collusion, and masculinized solidarity among workers—fosters and enforces a band-of-brothers mentality.
They're proudly working to protect the jobs of their white brothers and fighting to produce new jobs for their white brothers.
It's harder to tell if the mob is racist.
Probably.
You would think so.
At least, I think so.
I assume so without knowing anything about it.
And I'm almost certainly right.
But there's also a way in which the mob might not care.
There are probably lots of things they don't care about.
For example, they definitely don't care about environmental issues.

And they might not care who works for them.
They're more interested in controlling the ports.

Zach was raised in a tense family situation.
His parents don't want to get divorced, but they haven't spoken in twenty years.
They live in the same house.
His father lives on the second floor, and his mother lives on the ground floor.
They have an unwritten schedule for coming and going, and for using the kitchen, so they don't run into each other.
Maybe this situation is not as tense for them as I imagine it.
Maybe they're used to it.
Maybe something about it is even comforting.
Maybe it's comforting to know that the other person wants to avoid conflict as much as you do.
Maybe there's no potential for conflict, even though the situation suggests that conflict is always lingering, that coming down the stairs a few minutes too early or too late could result in a confrontation.
Maybe when they do accidentally see each other they simply mumble and look away and move on, and maybe it's nice when that happens, they silently feel good about it, they feel like they understand each other.
Maybe that's the best part of their day.

When they need to communicate, they leave little notes around the house.

Please sign these documents.

I'm saving this magazine, don't throw it away.

The pantry light is out.

"I visited them last weekend," Zach said, "and I found a note from my father to my mother explaining that she shouldn't hire someone to fix the garage door because he's already ordered parts to fix it, and then it details how she should open the garage if needed and which parts he's buying.

The note is dated '5/4,' but neither of them seemed to know which year it was written.

The door's been broken for a long time, but it doesn't matter because the garage is full of junk, you couldn't put a car in there, there's no reason to open the door.

"After they're dead, I imagine we'll gradually find more notes that maybe the other one never even saw.

Hahaha.

We'll also probably find a bunch of little notes that my mother writes each year for our 'Easter egg scavenger hunt,' these meandering, stream-of-consciousness clues that are riddled with inside jokes and never point clearly to the hiding place, so she usually includes a parenthetical at the end that just says where to look."

Some of the more idealistic young folks in the environmental activist groups probably think that the labor unions actually care about environmental issues; they think labor is an unqualified good and that unions are inherently progressive.

But the more experienced activists know that there's a quiet struggle between themselves and labor because environmental regulations can drive up costs, which can make it harder for labor to negotiate their wages, and so developers are able to play these groups against each other.

This is one reason the unions need the mob, because developers are very powerful.

But, of course, sometimes the mob is affiliated with a developer too.

This makes tracking the motivations of any individual group extremely difficult.

None of them are entirely discrete organizations.

There's overlap.

You'd be surprised at how this connects to the school board.

"Sure, it can get violent.

Sometimes the mob reacts severely to things you wouldn't expect them to even notice.

And sometimes it's unclear what they're reacting to.

They're just aggressive morons.

That's why you have to be careful.

That's why I worry about telling you this.

Not that I know anything about mob killings.

I don't know anything about that.
No, I don't hear about that kind of thing.
I've never heard of that.
I'm just speculating.
That's total speculation."

*

From what I can tell, I take long showers.
But I don't spend much time washing.
Often I only wash a few parts of myself.
Not necessarily the same few parts.
First I stand under the hot water for a few minutes looking down
blankly at my stomach and legs.
I don't wet my hair right away.
Maybe I think about something that I already regret saying last
night.
Maybe I obsess over how I could have phrased it differently, and I
get a little defensive on my own behalf—it was hard to express, of
course it came out wrong, what can they expect, what can I expect,
it's not as if there's a script for saying things exactly right, everyone
makes mistakes, everyone says things they shouldn't, why should
I bother regretting it, it's stupid to dwell on this, I should just let it
go, it's no big deal, I can't believe I'm still thinking about this, I can't
believe I said that, it might have been really hurtful, why did I say
that, what was I thinking, why can't I keep my fucking mouth shut.

Eventually I scrub an armpit.
I stretch one arm over my head and hold my palm against the
moldy shower wall and lather for longer than necessary, for almost
a minute or two.

Then I scrub the other armpit.

The skin in my armpits has been flaky and itchy for a while now, maybe a few years, on and off.

I wonder if this is caused by my deodorant, or if it's biological or environmental.

I wonder this almost every morning.

I close my eyes and wash my face.

I pass the soap over my belly and shoulders and arms.

I almost never soap my feet or ankles or legs.

Yellow dust falls from my ceiling.

My desk gets covered in this grainy dust and I wipe it clean every few days.

I actually don't know if *dust* is the right word.

It looks more like sand.

And it's not a uniform yellow—it's more like light brown and dark brown and yellow mixed with black specks.

But it feels like yellow is the dominant color.

Sometimes when I'm falling asleep, I think about the yellow dust.

Specifically, I think: will breathing the yellow dust while I sleep make me sick?

And then I think: has breathing the yellow dust while I sleep already made me sick?

How sick am I?

Was it ok to invite my girlfriend Ida to stay with me for a week when there's yellow dust falling out of the ceiling?

What was I thinking?

What if, years from now, she suddenly experiences a shock of terrible abdominal pain and falls to the ground and we call an ambulance and the doctors can't find anything wrong and the pain passes and it never happens again but I secretly can't stop wondering to myself if it's the sign of something worse and I'm sure she's wondering the same thing?

How many nights can she sleep here before it's dangerous?

Is even one night dangerous?

I wish she were here right now, that we didn't live on separate continents.

I wish we were showering together.

I wish I were washing her hair, standing behind her while she hangs her head and scrunches her eyes and the water streams down her face and back and arms and I gather her heavy wet long hair in my hands and run my fingers through it until the shampoo is rinsed away.

There's a tiny dark window in the bathroom.

The glass is so dusty that light barely streams through.

We're a little shiny from the water and the soap.

I press myself against her.

When it's my turn to wash I pretend that I usually wash my whole body.

I pay special attention to my legs.

I scrub them with exaggerated thoroughness as she stands there waiting for her turn to get back under the water.

We chat.

She holds me from behind.

She kneads my head.

I raise my arm and she washes my armpit.

She has one arm around me.

She kisses my back.

I moan because it feels good to be kissed, to be washed, to be loved—and I want her to know how good it feels, but I moan softly, under my breath, and I don't know if she can hear it over the running water, so I do it again, just a little louder, and I don't know if she hears this time either.

*

I don't remember wanting to be rich.
I don't remember moving to this city with dreams of living in a
spacious loft with one piece of geometrically abstract art hanging
on each enormous bare white wall.

I'd leave one wall empty.
Or maybe I'd leave all the walls empty and the pipes exposed and
the beautiful wooden ceiling unfinished and I'd build tall wide
bookshelves and fill them with hardcover books and unusual
objects, really interesting objects, a mixture of antique curiosities
and sculptural works, and it would be hard at first glance to figure
out what's art and what's ornament, which would be part of the
point.
And I'd invite people over after art events.
I'd open my home to others.
Yes, of course, invite your friends, bring them along, all your
friends are welcome.
Everyone's welcome.
I'd greet strangers and make them feel at home.
I'd offer them a glass a wine.
I'd see someone standing awkwardly by the bookshelves because
they don't know many people here and they feel out of place and
unused to being in the homes of the wealthy; they're excited to
be here but a little unsure of the etiquette and the conversations

seem intimidatingly casual so they're shyly hanging out near the books looking over the titles, rereading each spine a few times and wondering which objects are art, and I'd walk over and start chatting with them about my collection.

I'd show off a few of the kitschier pieces; I wouldn't say anything about the expensive art.

Then I'd graciously walk away and return to a conversation with an old friend, Charlotte, who'd be whispering to another old friend in the corner.

I'd ask her how she is.

She'd tell me that she recently learned her mother is schizophrenic and realized that she had actually known it for a long time.

The diagnosis retroactively clarified her mother's personality and behavior, which was both comforting and frightening, because now Charlotte feels like she can be more understanding, but has to come to grips with the fact that she had been living with the knowledge that her mother was ill without recognizing it directly or helping her find the proper care and medication.

Then she'd say that she'll tell me more about it soon, she doesn't want to talk about it now, we should get a drink sometime later this week.

The bedroom door would be open, and my guests will have piled their coats on my bed.

I can't decide whether to install marble countertops.

On the one hand, they're easy to clean and they keep the kitchen cool.

And I love how white marble reflects and amplifies light.

But on the other hand, marble is susceptible to staining.

It's a porous stone, and has a chemical structure that reacts easily with acids (for example, lemon juice or turmeric) and leads to etching on the surface.

There are basically two ways to treat marble countertops to protect them, and there are pros and cons to both methods.

You could get a honed finish, which involves sanding the surface until it's soft and matte.

A honed finish won't show scratches as much, but the stone is less bright and stains easily, so you have to seal it regularly, either professionally or by buying a sealer and doing it yourself.

If you spill something that etches the surface, which will almost certainly happen if you cook regularly, you can try to get the etching out by making a paste of baking soda and water, spreading it over the marble, covering it with cling wrap, and taping it down for two days.

This should pull out the mark.

The other kind of treatment is a polished finish, which is shinier, brighter, and stains less easily, but is much more easily scratched.

But polished marble wears down in time, so some people recommend that if you prefer the worn look you should just go straight to a honed finish.

When I met Charlotte for a beer she told me more about her mother.

"She's probably been schizophrenic for a long time.

She's paranoid, she rants about things that don't make sense, makes a lot of negative statements, talks about how people are evil, says random dark shit.

She's obsessed with violence, she sometimes talks about scalping techniques.

You know, how to cut someone's scalp off.

You know what I mean.

So when I learned she was schizophrenic, all of her previous behavior started to make more sense.

"Guess how I found out?

One day I got a text from my dad at 9 a.m. on a Wednesday morning that said, 'Oh, I forgot to tell you about your mother's psychotic break.'

Hahaha.

He had been in denial.

For example, my mother had been hearing things, but my dad had assumed that the equipment for her sleep apnea was picking up radio waves and somehow transmitting them to her; he had decided that she was just hearing the radio.

He was doing some wishful thinking.

"She thought that the government had bugged her house, and the neighbors were spying on her.

She found a piece of metal in the vent and was convinced that it was spy equipment.

And now she doesn't really leave her bedroom.
My dad is stuck at home most of the time too, taking care of her.

"I was never close to her because she's always been strange.
And so I've never tried to talk to her about her mental health.
I usually just ask her how she is, and then I pause in a way that's
meant to let her know that I'm concerned for her, but she doesn't
seem to pick up on that.
Or maybe she knows exactly what I'm doing but decides not to
respond.
It's hard to tell.

"She doesn't deal with anything directly.
My dad mediates the world for her, he wouldn't let me ask a blunt
question because he knows it would upset her and he wants to
protect her from that.
He would probably interrupt the conversation by kissing the top of
her head.
That would be a signal for me to stop talking, hahaha.
He's always kissing the top of her head.

"But it would be good to figure out how to talk to her, because now
that she stopped drinking my dad started drinking, and the last
time I visited I found him passed out in my mom's room, on her
bed.
He never goes in there, hahaha.

I should probably be in better touch with her.

Just in case.

But even if I worked up the courage to start a serious conversation, it would still be hard because she's really dissociative, she changes the subject without context.

I think her inability to segue or contextualize feeds her paranoia. Maybe it's one of the big things that makes her paranoid, because no one understands her and then she gets frustrated."

*

Recently, while lying in bed and breathing yellow dust, I watched a choppy, pixelated download of Valérie Massadian's film *Nana*.

The first half follows a four-year-old girl as she hangs around while her parents and grandparents work on their pig farm: they bleed a pig, they collect firewood, they set a rabbit trap.

In the second half of the film, the adults disappear, and Nana finishes the chores herself.

She unsnags the dead rabbit and carries it back to the house.

She cleans up.

She collects more sticks.

She starts a fire and cooks the rabbit.

Apparently, Massadian didn't script the film, and she didn't write lines for the child actor.

Instead, she collaborated with the kid on ideas for situations, and then filmed her saying whatever she wanted.

There's a great scene in which Nana is sitting alone on a bench putting a puzzle together and talking to herself in the voices of her parents.

"What a fucking mess.

What a big fucking mess.

I'm sick of your bullshit.

You think you're so smart.

You're full of crap.

I'm sick and tired of her crap."

Nana is about how work and knowledge are transmitted intergenerationally, and that's interesting, but this moment is especially moving because the actor's literal work—acting—involves repeating things she's presumably heard from her real-life parents.

She's already learned so much about adult psychology.

She already knows that love involves repeatedly performing your bitterness about the world as if it were bitterness about your loved one, as if your loved one were the center of the world, until the bitterness really does become about your loved one and then folds back into the love you have for them so that the love feels like it's deepening or doubling (or some other metaphor for abstract intensification) and your loved one seems even more central—doubly central—to the world as you know it.

Ida told me a funny story about her son.

At two years old, he's too young to watch superhero movies, and he's never seen one, but is nonetheless completely fixated on superheroes, which he learned about by watching older boys play.

He wants to wear costumes all the time.

It's hard to get him to wear anything else.

But he's also learned to fight and hit, because that's what he sees older boys do when they play superhero games.

I found this surprising.

It's not surprising that codes of gendered behavior are transmitted culturally at a young age, but it's surprising that popular movies are so incredibly effective at transmitting these codes that they don't even need to be seen.

Of course, he doesn't really want to hurt anyone, and he doesn't really want to be heroic.

He's a happy kid, and happiness is repetitive, imitative.

He likes to tell me that I'm dumb.

He likes to repeat: "Steve is dumb, Steve is dumb."

And I like to repeat it back to him: "Steve is dumb, Steve is dumb."

When I was a boy I compulsively told my parents I loved them.

I still have that compulsion; I tell Ida I love her so frequently that she often responds, "I know, you tell me all the time."

But then I say it again anyway.

I wish I were holding her hand in a department store right now.

I wish she and I were shopping for a kitchen countertop for our new home.

I wish we were standing side by side and her arm was around my waist and we were pointing at different patterns of marbled laminate.

This one will match the walls.

Yeah, but this one will match the curtains.

It doesn't matter if it matches the curtains, we can just get new curtains.

Well, we can repaint the walls too.

I don't want to repaint the walls, that's a lot of work.

Good point, I don't want to do that either.

This one is nice.

That one is nice, I agree, but it's not my favorite.

It's not my favorite either, but I like how the marble pattern has a little green in it, but you really only notice it if you look closely.

Oh yeah, that's nice.

And I don't think it will scratch easily.

No, I don't think it will.

So we can cut things right on it.

I don't know if we should do that, we should probably still use a cutting board, even if it doesn't scratch easily.

I'm not saying we don't ever need to use a cutting board, I'm just saying that if we run out of space on the cutting board and we use the countertop, it probably won't be a big deal.

Yeah, I understand what you're saying.

Oh, I thought you misunderstood, I thought you thought I was saying that we could just use the countertop as a replacement for a cutting board all the time.

No, I understood what you were saying.

Ok.

Ok, well, let's go home and think about this, I'm getting hungry.

Well, first I have to stop at the grocery store, we're out of dish soap.

That sounds good, there're some things I want to pick up, too.

Let's grab a bottle of wine, we can drink it later tonight.

Oh yeah, that's a great idea.

*

My friend Jordan told me a funny story about Heath Ledger's death.
He was walking around Soho and happened to pass the luxury
apartment building where Ledger overdosed.
There were a few hundred people lingering outside.
Jordan approached a woman at the back of the crowd and asked her
what was going on.
"Heath Ledger died," she said.
Then she paused and added, "I'm glad he's dead."

*

I met my friend Lydia for a beer, and she told me about her new
relationship.
He lives abroad, he's forty years her senior, and he makes her very
happy, even though it's difficult to live so far apart.
She's heartened and excited by their ability to manage unhappiness,
to talk openly about intractable problems.

She said: "In some couples, you have this wind shear effect.
What I mean is, both of you can have intense fears but the fears are
not complementary.
Wind shear, that's the word.
You don't know that word?
I always forget what it means.
I've looked it up several times.
It has something to do with physics, you know, two things that are
very strong that move past each other in opposite directions and
affect each other.
Something to do with air pressure.
Two things come into contact and this creates friction, tension,
something like that.

"Anyway, you know, moving outside of the metaphor, we
just have these moments of recognizing that we haven't been
communicating.

When we slow down, we realize that something we may have been very scared of doesn't have a home in the other person.

"But no, I wasn't scared of getting together with someone older than me.
And I was thinking about this recently—about how I wasn't scared—because he and I were talking about death, actually.
We have to talk about it.
We can't ignore that conversation.
I mean, it's not like we think about it every day, but we also don't want to repress it.
Because, you know, it's real, and there's real grief in it for me.
I mean, something could happen and we could go our separate ways in two weeks.
But assuming that doesn't happen, I don't think I've ever experienced the limit of human life like this before.
It's simple: it's impossible that he'll know me when I'm the age he is now.
And so, in a way, his age gives us access to—or it allows us to live in—a different kind of time, an urgent kind of time, but actually that urgent kind of time is what we should be living in anyway.
But we can't, because life is exhausting.

"I mean, for all I know, I'll drop dead in a few months.
Listen, Steve.
In the last three or four days, I've heard of three people dropping dead.

One guy my age of an aneurysm.

One woman, a friend of a friend downstairs, she was about 50, she just died in her sleep overnight.

And another one I can't remember.

And so all of the sudden, it seemed like the world was calling on us to address the question of death, and that's why we were talking about it again.

I mean, sure, anyone could fall ill, anyone could drop dead, I could drop dead tomorrow.

But it's more likely for an older person.

I wonder why I'm not more perturbed by this stuff.

"Maybe because my mother died when my sister was still a teenager, and so I became a half-mom, and while I was learning to be a half-mom I was also dealing with legal stuff in Greece. Maybe that was good practice, or good experience, in taking care of others, or just dealing with shit.

But listen.

Listen, Steve.

My father is 65, and he's not particularly healthy, but somehow he's constitutionally hearty in a way I'm not.

I'm just not.

It probably has to do with growing up in a Greek fishing village. You know, he didn't wear shoes, breathed the air, was kind of a peasant, lived outdoors.

You know.

There's a certain heartiness in people who are a lot older and who lived outside, got more sun, didn't wear shoes, didn't consume as many hormones, who knows.

So what I'm saying about loving someone older than me is, that for someone older than me, he's actually very sturdy.

He has way more energy than I do.

"It's one of those things.

If something happens tomorrow, maybe I would fall apart.

Maybe I'd run away.

I don't know.

But all you have at your disposal is everything you've already lived, your experience and memory.

That's it, and either it's sufficient or it's not."

That's not quite what wind shear is.

I looked it up later.

According to weatherquestions.com, the term refers to an unpredictable shift in wind speed or direction over horizontal or vertical distances, which can cause a rapid change in lift and altitude for aircraft.

So Lydia's metaphor doesn't really work, but I like metaphors that don't work.

They bring distant things together without subsuming one into the other, amplifying their differences while establishing a skewed relation.

Even better, this metaphor also fails by working too well: it could be applicable to most any situation.

It's simultaneously obvious and abstruse: you know what she's saying about how misunderstandings evolve from lopsided communication, and yet it's hard to draw any specific insights from the comparison between human love relationships and weather.

That's why I like it so much.

It reaffirms a general idea, but inconclusively.

As if abstract generalizations could be real and true, but only as details in stories traversed with other details—some of which cluster together as if seeking commonality, and some of which float away.

*

In the 1958 film *The Blob*, Steve McQueen plays a moody teenager who accidentally discovers an amoeboidal alien life-form that grows enormous as it envelops and absorbs people and objects.
One of the best parts of the movie is that McQueen's performance is a barely disguised imitation of James Dean: he fidgets and spazzes, a tight knot of angsty confusion and aimless energy.
Of course, McQueen is much less brilliant than Dean, but his bad nervy version of a teenager might be an even truer rendering of male adolescence because of how unselfconsciously gawky its theatrics are.
Far from Dean's graceful anxiety, his movements are reactive and malicious.
His character dramatizes shame as a way of foisting it onto others: he seems to want everyone to be as awkward and angry as himself.

Eager to share this observation, I talked about it to my friendTeddy at a party.
But I could quickly tell that either he wasn't listening, or my mildly counterintuitive point about *The Blob* didn't impress him.
So I dropped the subject and asked how he was doing.
Pretending that I could understand his reply over the loud music, I started to talk about another movie, because he likes movies, when suddenly he stumbled and grabbed a fistful of my hair and leaned

in close to my face and said something vaguely threatening or prophetic like, "I know you're in there."

It was immediately clear that he had been hiding his drunkenness since the conversation began, had been attempting to listen, or to appear like he was listening.

I don't know how he'll get home.

One of our friends will put him in a cab and his girlfriend will find him leaning against their apartment door.

I can see her attempting to coax him to bed, unbuttoning his shirt, tugging at his shoes.

I can see him pushing her away.

Maybe she'll leave him on the floor.

He'll wake up half-dressed, still drunk.

He won't be able to find his shirt.

Where did you put my shirt?

Where's my shirt?

Where's my fucking shirt?

Ow, fuck.

Fuck this table.

I hate this table.

It's always fucking covered in shit.

Why is it always fucking covered in shit?

What is this shit?

These aren't mine.

These magazines aren't mine.
Do you think I'm ever going to read this shit?
National Geographic?
Seriously? *National Geographic?*
Who reads this?
Throw this shit out.
Will somebody throw this shit out?
I don't want it.
I never fucking wanted it.
It's not mine.
Where the fuck is my shirt?
Where did you put it?
That's not it.
I said that's not fucking it.
That's not my fucking shirt either.
No, it's not.
I said it's not, it's fucking not.
I said it's fucking not.

But Teddy doesn't talk like this.
Not at all.
He's much quieter and more enigmatic—gentle and oblique.
I've never heard him attempt to verbally wound or sting someone
else, and I've never heard him raise his voice.
So I have no idea what his anger or frustrated confusion would look
like.

I can't quite imagine it.

There are a few entries in Judith Malina's diaries where she attempts to understand my great-uncle Dick's sadness.

She's clearly struggling to empathize with her distressed friend, who suffers from the memories of his time in jail, and who expresses pain variously: sometimes in depressive self-pity, sometimes in bitter outbursts, and sometimes in levelheaded—but strained—words of wisdom.

On August 1, 1951, she wrote:

> Dicken is suffering from his prison experience, though he's never spoken much about it.
>
> 'I was young,' he would say, 'and when one is young one can stand a great deal that would be unbearable in later years.' But now he talks about prison because he feels imprisoned in our house, feels his room intolerably cell-like, and sleeps instead in the studio.
>
> He speaks of his analysis as a period of waiting which he confuses with his prison term, feeling he's doing 'bad time.'
>
> His experiences in the prison strike in Chillicothe and in solitary fill me with premonition, fear that draws no line between anticipation and memory.
>
> The worst moment for prisoners, he says, is the moment before the door shuts for the night.

A few weeks later, on August 19, 1951, she wrote about Dick's prison experience again.

She had a nightmare about a home invasion.

The dream is claustrophobic.

It's as if her unconscious was trying to relate to—or comprehend in a metaphor—his sense of isolation:

> A terrifying dream: I have told Dicken a secret and this knowledge has been discovered by a band of criminals. They have imprisoned us in our house; there are many other people, but they cannot help us. The criminals have a mysterious, immaterial murder device, a psychological method of killing with a look and a touch. The victim slowly loses his willpower; no matter what he does he will wither and die in a few hours.
>
> Our four captors are jazz musicians. Their leader is a handsome man who wears a metal band on his head which holds a jackknife.
>
> Julian searches wildly through some school notes which, he claims, contain a remedy, a simple antidote.
>
> I can't bear to watch Dicken's slow death, and blurt out that I'm going to call the police. The handsome gangster comes toward me, touches my shoulder, looks into my eyes as with deep tenderness, smiles, and says, 'Now you have it too.'

I panic. We await death in Dicken's room. I see myself in a large mirror, half my hair dyed yellow. Remy, too, is there under the influence of this spell. Julian, who has some kind of immunity, suddenly finds the answer: light and cold water. As simple as that. A kind of awakening and ablution. We put on all the lights. I wash my face. I feel less numb. We go to rescue Dicken who is still in his room in the dark. He is slumped over. Asleep? I am terrified.

Julian awakens me. Even now, I'm shaken. For hours I panic when anyone turns the lights off.

*

Last night, Ida and I lay in bed lazily rubbing our warm feet on each other's legs and whispering sweet things about how wonderful the day had been.
It was such a good day.
I had such a good day with you.
The best day.
I loved everything about it.
It was so good.
I especially loved the morning.
I love having breakfast with you.
I want to have breakfast with you every morning.

I asked her to tell me a story, and she told me about how white asparagus is grown.
In her early 20s, Ida spent a few months working on a farm in Washington State.
She said, "White asparagus is more expensive than green asparagus and takes a little more work to produce.
It's a luxury item, a vegetable grown almost exclusively for high-end restaurants.
It's not a real vegetable.
Well, it's a real vegetable, of course it's real—but the way we farm it, it's so labor-intensive and ridiculous.

"You only plant asparagus once, and then at the end of the season they fern.

Have you ever seen an asparagus grow?

When it stops being asparagus it becomes a fern, and you have to let that happen once a year at the end of the season.

I don't really know why, to be totally honest.

I was just told that that's what happens, and my knowledge of the science behind plants is limited to a sort of generalists' knowledge.

"But the thing I learned about farming is that once you know how to do it, 'why' is not a really important question.

It's just pragmatics.

If that's what it takes to get more asparagus, you don't need to know why.

I'm sure the farmer I worked for knew 'why' at some point, but he had clearly forgotten.

"Anyway, asparagus is planted in long rows, and at the beginning of the season, you can see the tip of the spear starting to poke its head out.

So we would begin by taking a truck and filling it with hay and metal hoops and a couple of pitchforks, and we would drive up the hill in the farmer's pickup truck.

His name was Matt.

"So me and Matt would pitchfork the hay onto the field, and then we'd drive a little bit further and throw the hay off the back of the truck and spread it around.
The hay damps down the weeds.
This was an organic farm so we weren't using any pesticides, so you need the hay to kill the weed growth.

"So then we'd find the rows of asparagus, and you'd take these hoops and drop about ten down near one row.
Every five or ten feet you would just drop a hoop and stick it in the ground.
We would spend all day laying these hoops along the rows.
We put hundreds of hoops down, literally hundreds, and then we'd cover it all with a tarp.

"You can't let the asparagus head hit the tarp, because the spear will get blunted off from the heat and friction.
And asparagus without a tightly wound head drops in price.

"So we would take two huge tarps and lay them on top of the hoops, and then put tractor tires on top to weigh it down.
The tarps create a greenhouse-type environment, they keep out the sunlight.
The reason you don't want sunlight, and the reason something's white, is that when a plant is fixing chlorophyll, through photosynthesis, it's creating plastids called chloroplasts.

And if it can't fix chlorophyll through photosynthesis, it'll get all its nutrients from the ground instead, and the plastid, instead of making chloroplasts in the cell, makes what are called etioplasts.

"It's a process called etiolation, have you ever heard that word before? When something's etiolated, it becomes a little blander, it becomes a little bit more tender, it becomes a little bit elongated, and also it's white.
So when you look at a leek, or a fennel bulb, you can see where the leek was in the ground and where it wasn't in the ground.
Do you see what I'm saying?
You can literally see that delineation within the plastid.
There's a different cellular structure from where it's white to where it's green.
It's made of different parts, even though it's a coherent plant.

"Anyway, so Matt didn't have a lot of people working for him.
He had me and these two older people.
Normally we'd all be in the field picking asparagus at our own paces.
We picked by hand.
When you buy asparagus, sometimes it's hard at the bottom, and that's because they have a machine that picks asparagus, it just digs into the ground.
But when you snap it with your hand—it's really painful, because you have to sit with your back arched, holding a basket, for hours a day—you don't get that hard part at the bottom.

"So when the time came, Matt and I would throw all the tractor tires off the tarps on one side of the field.

And then the two older people would start picking the asparagus on that side, while me and Matt would throw the tires off the other side of the other tarp and start to pull that back as well.

Because the thing about white asparagus is that it wants to be green. It wants to eat better.

You're starving this thing and it wants to eat, and if it eats it will start turning green within about a half hour, and when it does you've lost about two or three dollars a pound, the minute it changes color.

"And so as soon as we pulled the tarp back they would start to pick, and we would come help them, and when they were done we'd immediately throw the tarp back on.

And sometimes—because it was on a hill, and it was really windy— these tarps would become like sails.

You'd be throwing tractor tires on, and then this gust of wind would get caught under the tarp and you'd watch the tires you had just put down flip right off.

There were days when me and Matt couldn't get a single tarp down. Although one day when it was really windy we were lucky.

Some guy came to visit Matt, and we got him to help us pull the tarps down, because the wind was gusting so hard that you just couldn't do anything at all."

Acknowledgements

Earlier versions of some sections of *Honestly* were published in a chapbook by Kenning editions, and in Total Effekt's *Living Magasine*. I would like to thank the editors. And special thanks to Aaron Winslow for all his careful reading and astute criticism.

Steven Zultanski is the author of several books of poetry, most recently *Bribery* (2014). His critical writing has appeared in *4 Columns, Art in America, frieze*, the *Los Angeles Review of Books, Mousse*, and elsewhere. In January 2017, an art exhibition inspired by his book *Agony* (published by BookThug in 2012), entitled *You can tell I'm alive and well because I weep continuously*, was shown at the Knockdown Center in Queens. He lived for many years in New York City but now resides in Copenhagen, Denmark.

Colophon

Manufactured as the first edition of *Honestly*
in the Spring of 2018 by Book*hug.

Distributed in Canada by the
Literary Press Group: lpg.ca

Distributed in the USA by
Small Press Distribution: spdbooks.org

Shop on-line at bookthug.ca

BOOK
PRODUCTION
WAR ECONOMY
STANDARD

Type + design by Jay Millar
Edited for the press by Aaron Winslow
Copy-edited by Stuart Ross